A Primer On Pietism:

Its Characteristics and Inevitable Impact on the Christian Life

By

Ryan Haskins
Jeremy Litts
Jon Moffitt
Byron Yawn

Theocast, Inc.
P.O. Box 592
Nolensville, TN 37135
(615) 212-9212
www.theocast.org

ISBN-10: 0-692-91526-5

ISBN-13: 978-0-692-91526-4

To those people who were our constant motivation to keep moving ahead. We thank you for the clarity we received as a result of your efforts. We would never be here had you never been there.

There are too many to name.
You know who you are.

INTRODUCTION

The most common question we get concerns our use of the terms *pietism* and *confessionalism*. These two descriptors are in constant rotation among the boys of *Theocast*. Over the years, as we have sought to clarify and define our perspective, we have found these terms helpful. "We are not pietists" is the quickest route to who we are. We realize more technical definitions exist, and scholars could object to our broad application of the terms. We hope they will cut us some slack. They are, after all, within the proper boundaries of their general definitions. The meaning of these expressions (as we have employed them) are not mysterious to those who follow our ministry. Whether they've used the expression or not, most people know exactly what we mean when we say "pietists." For most, it's as if we are finally putting words to what they've been long thinking.

These two categories have proven extremely useful to us because they are specific enough to capture a single idea and broad enough to encompass large categories of thought. Or, to put that another way, they are specific enough to be obvious and general enough to include any number of realities. As we use them, the terms are intended to capture two very distinct ethos under which innumerable movements and perspectives exist.

✳ "There are two types of evangelicals out there: pietists and confessionalists." As we attempted to put our arms around general approaches to Protestant Christianity, these two labels were the largest we could find. We chose early on not to contrast ourselves with "fundamentalists" because this would be too narrow a classification. People can easily wiggle out of this label, or embrace it without taking on larger implications. As it is, fundamentalism is merely a small room in the massive edifice of pietism. While not everyone would identify as a fundamentalist, everyone can ✳ be identified in these larger paradigms. You can be a pietist without being a fundamentalist, but you can't be a fundamentalist without being a pietist. We realize the categories are not watertight, but generally you identify as one or the other. As it were.

What is certain is that our depiction of pietism has begun to resonate with a mass of people. "That's my experience" is a regular message we receive. For this we are very grateful. It is our prayer that as our ministry continues to grow and more people "join the reformation," more resources will become available. We thought it would be most helpful to begin with the basics. *A Primer on Pietism* is intended to catch people up on the conversation. We want you to walk away from this short little read and "get it." We pray it is helpful in this way. Also, when you get asked the same question we are asked ("What is pietism?") feel free to pass it on. Together, let's proselytize as many pietists as possible before Christ returns.

Post Tenebras Lux

June 26th, 2017
Nashville, TN
The Boys

BETWEEN SHOULD AND AM

Let's begin with terminology. What do we mean by "pietism"? We mean to identify that approach to Christianity that is preoccupied with the interior of the Christian life. We like to say pietism is characterized by an "inward orientation." This is not to say there aren't objective commitments (doctrine) within pietism. There are. But a commitment to the spirituality and moral progress of the individual Christian overwhelms pietism's messaging. There are other characteristics, but this is its main attribute. Progress in the Christian life is its *summum bonum. Should* is pietism's main focus. It is about what we *should* be doing, how we *should* go about doing it and where we *should be* as compared to *where we are*. Pietism specializes in pointing out the exact distance between *should* and *am*. It is concerned that we progress.

In the broadest sense the main focus of pietism is *the life of the Christian.* This observation is central. Pietism has committed itself to placing the *duty of the Christian* above all other realities. The real issue with pietism is not only what it emphasizes but also what it minimizes. The concern is not that Christ is missing from pietism's message. This would be an unfair characterization. The concern is rather that Christ's work stands more in the background than in the foreground (Colossians 2:20-23). This is seen clearly in that most all information and instruction within pietism is aimed at how to live. Duty overshadows identity. Pietism begins with the question, "What must I do?" In this schema *obligation* precedes *assurance*. As will be argued, this order of priorities leads to a confusion of theological categories and despair in the life of the believer.

When we refer to *pietism* we don't intend to deny the place of piety (godliness, transformation, etc.). Piety is a legitimate and important category in Christian theology (Colossians 3). We believe in piety. But to be clear, we don't believe (as pietists do) that piety is *the central concern* of Christianity. We also believe true piety results in a wholly different manner than pietism would suggest (we will get to this). Suffice it to say that piety and pietism are two different categories of thought. Pietism is an ideology that is preoccupied with piety. All its messages, materials and admonitions are dedicated to cultivating piety in the Christian life. Piety, on the other hand, is a quality produced in the believer by the Holy Spirit (Ezekiel 36:25-27).

Pietism (hyper-piety) is a very real, historic and identifiable phenomenon. It has most often shown up as a countermeasure to the opposite problem (hyper-orthodoxy). Whenever the attention of the church is turned singularly toward doctrine (orthodoxy), some fear a focus on Christian duty will be lost. Pietism is usually the collective response to this fear. Not surprisingly, pietism emerged prominently in the years following the German Reformation. Given the high concentration of theological distinction generated during this season, it's not hard to see how conditions were ripe for pietism. Certain characteristics within the modern expressions of pietism can be traced back to this moment. Anymore the presence of pietism within evangelicalism is ubiquitous. Evangelicalism is a pietistic movement.

BETWEEN FINISHED AND AM

In order to contrast our perspective with pietism, and distance ourselves from its confusion, we've come to identify ourselves as "confessionalists." This too is an identifiable category within Christian thought. We intend for "confessionalism" to carry the exact opposite accent of that found within pietism. The emphasis in confessionalism is altogether in an opposite direction. Confessionalism is an "outwardly focused" orientation. *Done* is its main emphasis. It is primarily about what has been *accomplished by another* and how we go about benefiting from this accomplishment (Romans 5:1-5; Ephesians 2:4-10). It is concerned that we are always grasping our standing before God despite where we might be at any given moment. Confessionalism specializes in proclaiming the relationship between *finished* and *am*. It is finished. I am a child of God. This is not to say there aren't practical elements (piety) within confessionalism. There are. But a commitment to keeping the finished work of Christ at the center of the believer's focus overwhelms confessionalism's messaging (2 Peter 1:9). There are other characteristics, but this is its main attribute. Therefore, the core of this perspective is Christ and not the Christian.

In the broadest sense the main focus of confessionalism is *the life of Christ*. This observation is central. Confessionalism is committed to placing *the accomplishment of Christ* above all other realities. The Christian life stands in the background and is only rightly understood when Christ is in the foreground. This is seen clearly in that most information and instruction within confessionalism is aimed at describing what God has accomplished in and through Christ. Confessionalism proclaims the *Good News* and promotes those effects that inevitably flow from it. Christ has done (past) all that is necessary to secure God's favor and approval on the sinner's behalf (present/future). Confessionalism asks the question, "Who am I?" In this schema *assurance* precedes *duty*. As will be argued, this order of priorities clears the way for a life of freedom and joy. Compared to the theological chaos that lies outside its walls, we have found a balanced and reasonable faith within the confines of confessionalism. We have found a faith that places the stress on the divine love of God rather than the imperfect efforts of the weary pilgrim.

The etymology of "confessionalism" is self-evident. It's a tip of the hat to the historic confessions of the Reformed church that have chalked the field of orthodoxy over the centuries. Therefore, "confessionalism" is marked by the same theological consistency and emphasis that typifies the Reformed tradition. To "confess" a truth is to acknowledge or declare one's commitment to that truth. Confessions, therefore, represent the unified commitment of the Reformed church to a body of doctrine drawn from the Bible.

At various times in the church's history a clarification of theological categories was a necessary antidote to aberrant theology. Usually, confessions were born in moments of theological crisis. In particular - those confessions born out of the Reformation were a direct response to the moralism that systematically overwhelmed the church. At a time when Christianity was completely focused on the morality of the saint (cooperating with the church), some feared that the singular place of Christ's finished work would be lost. The Reformation was the collective response to this fear.

As a result, the focus of the Reformed confession is largely concerned with presenting the work of Christ (received by faith) as the exclusive basis of justification before God. This was in contrast to the synergistic works-righteousness system of the medieval church. All of this to say, the Reformed confessions are primarily "outwardly focused." Generally, they trend in an opposite direction of pietism and moralism. Christ's work precedes that of the Christian. While much of the Reformed confessions deal directly and carefully with the Christian life, the motivation for piety is never outside the footprint of what Christ has already accomplished (Colossians 3:12-17).

OF VERY DIFFERENT TONES

On a practical level the differences between pietism and confessionalism are numerous. The distinctions, while not being exclusive to either, flow from the central commitments of each perspective. The following qualities naturally flow from each viewpoint:

- Pietism is heavily practical in nature (do). Confessionalism is heavily declarative in nature (done).

- They are of very different tones. Because pietism is concerned with a reformation of behavior, its tone is usually exacting. Because confessionalism is concerned with the believer's confidence in Christ, its tone is usually compassionate.

- Since pietism is focused on what Christians *should do,* the Gospel is usually seen as the entry point for ongoing duty. Since confessionalism is focused on Christ's work, the Gospel is both the foundation of the sinner's confidence before God and the shelter under which they live in this fallen world.

- Pietism has a tendency to erode a sense of assurance by obsessing over relative degrees of personal righteousness. Confessionalism seeks to bolster assurance by pointing to the alien righteousness of Christ received by faith.

- In pietism doubt often emerges as an implicit motivation for godliness. In confessionalism certainty motivates the believer.

- One knows they are experiencing pietism when sermons contain sheer instruction, view the Gospel as a footnote, or apply it to the non-Christian at the end of the service. One knows they are experiencing confessionalism when the Gospel surrounds the entire service and is applied mainly to the redeemed.

- Pietism stresses the practice of "spiritual disciplines" as a means to spiritual growth. Confessionalism stresses the ordinary means of grace (Word, sacrament, prayer) in strengthening one's faith in Christ.

- Pietism is concerned with cultivating spirituality in the individual. Confessionalism is concerned with exalting Christ as the sole object of faith.

- Pietism views assurance as the pursuit of the Christian life. Confessionalism sees assurance as the essence of Christianity.

- Pietism points the Christian inward to their progress in personal holiness. Confessionalism points the Christian outward to the righteousness of Christ.

- Pietism mixes Law and Gospel. Confessionalism maintains a distinction between Law and Gospel.

- Pietism is mainly concerned with nominalism. Confessionalism is mainly concerned with moralism.

WHAT YOU DO & WHO YOU ARE

One of the more notable traits of pietism is its inherent confusion of theological categories. As has already been mentioned, one of the benefits of confessionalism is its theological consistency. Pietism, by nature, lacks doctrinal continuity and can tend to be all over the theological road. Since there is no unifying theological system among pietists, contradictions on essential points of theology are commonplace. This is not to suggest that confessional contexts are infallible. Confessions are, after all, secondary sources written by flawed men. But the time-tested nature of the Reformed confessions does create a system of checks and balances for the church. Countless Christians over the centuries have found great comfort in the clarity and reliability of these documents. Pietism has no such framework. Systematics are mainly an individual endeavor. This is why, within evangelicalism, individual personalities and not historic confessions determine the beliefs of large anonymous groups of people.

There is no place where this confusion is more manifest than with the doctrine of salvation. Due to this lack of theological continuity, categories become vague to the point of contradiction. Pietism has a tendency to confess and deny the same things at the same time. Because of its bent towards moralism, pietism struggles to maintain fidelity with the Reformed and Protestant reality of justification by grace through faith. While pietists do affirm the cardinal doctrine of justification, there is, at the very same time, a penchant for obscuring its meaning. This is because *how* you live is the ultimate ground for *who* you are. In confessionalism, by contrast, *who* you are *in Christ* is the ground for *how* you live (Hebrews 10:12-13, 19-25). This is much different within pietism. In the end, the genuineness of one's justification (positional) is made to depend upon the degree of one's sanctification (linear). Rather than living the Christian life from the perspective of status forward, it is lived from duty forward. *Who we are* is always tied to *what we do*, rather than *what we do* being derived from *who we are*.

This logic creates an unending loop of despair and doubt. Consistent with pietism - piety is motivated by making God's favor dependent on our moral commitment level. This is where the inconsistencies are inevitable and the reversal of priorities (Christian life over accomplishment of Christ) is most notable in its effect. Whenever *our life* precedes *His life* as the primary emphasis, very predictable problems arise. Pietism inevitably creates spiritual insecurity by forcing the saint to rely on varying degrees of sanctification as the ground of their assurance. When *what we do* (Christian life) precedes *who we are* (in Christ) this outcome is unavoidable.

FOOTNOTING SOLA FIDE

Because of its fear of nominalism and the ever-present possibility of moral laxity, pietism resists an unqualified commitment to *Sola Fide*. As a preventative measure against immorality, faith (Christ's work) and faithfulness (our work) are drawn together as tightly as possible. Just enough space is left between the two realities for it to qualify as Protestant. Whenever the ground of assurance (*person of Christ*) and the evidence of conversion (*transformation of our life*) are made indistinguishable, the believer can never find rest. Life is approached from a transactional standpoint. I get when I give. The results of this distortion are devastating to the hope of the believer (Romans 5:1). From this angle instruction will always sound like a way to earn God's favor rather than an invitation to enjoy the freedom of God's favor we already possess.

Confessionalism does not share pietism's obsession over transformation, nor is it fearful that an absence of external pressures will result in a shortage of sanctification. Within confessionalism, sanctification is both certain and varying. This is because the whole of salvation is an act of God in Christ through the Holy Spirit working within the frame of the regenerate sinner (Ephesians 2:8-10). Change is an inevitable consequence of the same predestinating grace (Romans 8:28-30) that caused our justification in the first place. The "progress" of sanctification over the whole of the Christian life is as certain as the declaration of justification that inaugurated it. It is no less inevitable than the glorification that will occur at its terminus. If it is of grace then there is no sense in which it will not come to pass. As Luther wrote, "God transforms those he redeems. Those he does not transform he leaves in the consequence of their sin."

Pietism cannot comprehend an obedience that flows naturally from the heart of the Christian and is motivated by assurance rather than fear. This is why it balks on *Sola Fide*. Ultimately, "faith alone" means that a person's justification before God is not based on anything a person does or doesn't do before or after God has declared them righteous. We cannot be saved by works before or after we have been justified by grace through faith (Galatians 2:19-21). When Paul spoke of faith he did so in contrast to works. This is the shift people come to feel in a confessional world. This is the zero gravity moment for those who leave pietism. Within pietism doubt drives the believer forward because justification is made to depend on the person. Within confessionalism freedom drives the Christian forward because justification lies completely outside of the individual (2 Corinthians 5:18). While we believe the Christian will inevitably obey God, our obedience is not the basis for our standing before Him. That which saves us is outside of us.

Once we understand these realities, the focus of our daily life changes dramatically. Pietism drives the believer forward by the application of discipline in an effort to increase spiritual activity and godliness. We get through giving. When we lapse into sin, or struggle with our remaining corruption, we are cast into despair. This is inevitable since our confidence depends on our progress. Confessionalism invites the believer to set their focus on the Divine Love of the Father. He justified us through His son. He adopted us. He sanctifies us. He will safely bring us home. This is the constant refrain of the Gospel. "You are mine." The believer fights daily against the temptation to rest in their own righteousness rather than the righteousness of Christ. We fight daily to lay aside the entanglements that lead away from faith in Christ. As the church gathers, we are called to rest from our weariness as we rest in Christ (Hebrews 4:10-11). We are abiding with those abiding in Christ Jesus. We take up Christ's "body" and "blood" to remind us of our justification and adoption by grace. Our Father graciously bids us come. It's here that wrath and mercy meet in the person and work of Christ. The believer rests in the Father's arms instead of laboring to climb into them. We rest knowing our status is forever fixed. "God is good with you."

For additional resources and information, visit
Theocast.org

Made in the USA
San Bernardino, CA
29 August 2017